VETERINARY ADVICE ON

COLIC

IN HORSES

Tim Mair
BVSc, PhD, DEIM, DESTS, DipECEIM, MRCVS

ABOUT THE AUTHOR

Tim Mair has a special interest in the treatment of colic. After qualifying as a veterinary surgeon from the University of Bristol in 1980, he spent two years in general practice before returning to the University of Bristol to undertake research in equine respiratory disease.

After gaining a PhD in 1986, Tim became a lecturer in equine internal medicine. He went back into equine practice in 1990, and is currently a partner in the Bell Equine Veterinary Clinic in Kent.

Tim's main interests are equine internal medicine and soft tissue surgery.

ACKNOWLEDGEMENTS

Viv Rainsbury: illustrations (pages 6, 8, 15).
Tim Mair: photography (pages 3, 16, 18, 19, 22, 24, 28, 30, 33, 42).

Published by Ringpress Books, a division of Interpet Publishing, Vincent Lane, Dorking, Surrey, RH4 3YX, UK. Tel: 01306 873822   Fax: 01306 876712 email: sales@interpet.co.uk

First published 2004
© 2004 Ringpress Books. All rights reserved.

ISBN 1 86054 242 5

Printed and bound in Singapore by Kyodo Printing

10 9 8 7 6 5 4 3 2 1

CONTENTS

Introduction

The purpose of this book is to give the horse owner some basic information about colic, its causes, and its treatment. It is not intended as a 'home-doctoring' manual. Colic must always be considered as a potentially serious disease, and, in all but the most minor of episodes, professional attention from a qualified veterinary surgeon should be sought.

Colic is a common problem. To many horse owners, it conjures up thoughts of a serious, potentially fatal disease. Often, the word 'colic' is equated with 'twisted gut'. In reality, colic is simply a symptom indicative of abdominal pain, specifically pain arising from within the gastrointestinal tract. It is neither a diagnosis nor a single disease. Indeed, colic can be caused by many hundreds of different diseases. It can happen to any horse at any time.

Severe bouts of colic can be caused by serious, life-threatening diseases, and it may be necessary to carry out aggressive forms of treatment (sometimes involving surgery) early in the course of the disease, in order to save the animal. Colic, as a group of diseases, probably kills more horses than any other disease or even old age.

Fortunately, most horses showing signs of colic are affected by mild, benign forms of disease, which respond rapidly to simple treatments, or may even improve spontaneously. That said, even the very mild forms should never be ignored – conditions that produce mild signs of colic may progress to more severe forms of colic in a relatively short period of time.

1 Equine anatomy and colic

Before we approach colic itself, it is necessary to look at equine anatomy to understand how colic affects the horse.

ALIMENTARY TRACT

- **Mouth:** The horse evolved as a grazing herbivore. Its teeth enable it to pick up grass and to grind down food into a digestible consistency. As the cheek teeth grind, they become worn. The continuous eruption and grinding down of the teeth can result in the formation of sharp points, if the upper and lower teeth do not meet one another precisely. This can predispose the animal to some types of colic.
- **Oesophagus:** Once food is swallowed, it passes down the oesophagus (gullet), a muscular tube, to the stomach. Blockage of the oesophagus occasionally occurs (called choke), usually caused by a mass of food that gets stuck somewhere along its length. It is characterised by repeated retching by the horse, with discharge of saliva and food down the nose and out of the mouth.
- **Stomach:** The horse has a relatively small, simple stomach (rather like our own). The internal lining of the stomach has two separate regions: glandular and non-glandular. The former secretes hydrochloric acid, an important part of digestion (although it can occasionally predispose the horse to ulcers). The line of division between the two areas is called the margo plicatus. Ulcers often arise close to this line.
- **Small intestines:** From the stomach, food passes

THE EQUINE DIGESTIVE SYSTEM

STOMACH

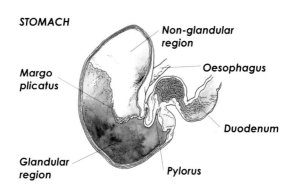

- Non-glandular region
- Oesophagus
- Margo plicatus
- Duodenum
- Glandular region
- Pylorus

GASTRO-INTESTINAL TRACT

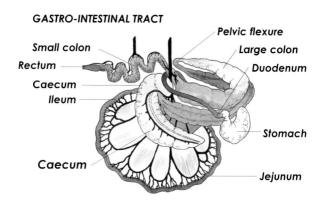

- Small colon
- Rectum
- Caecum
- Ileum
- Pelvic flexure
- Large colon
- Duodenum
- Stomach
- Caecum
- Jejunum

CAECUM

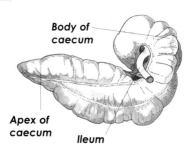

- Body of caecum
- Apex of caecum
- Ileum

through the small intestine, taking about two to four hours for food to pass. During this time, soluble carbohydrates and fats are digested.

The first part of the small intestine is called the duodenum. It is a horseshoe-shaped tube, about 3-5 feet (1-1.5 metres) long. The second, and longest, part of the small intestine is the jejunum. It is 55-92 feet (17-28 metres) long. The final part of the small intestine, the ileum, is 2-2.5 feet (0.7-0.8 metres) long, and has a thicker muscular wall than the duodenum or jejunum. It ends at a valve-like opening that projects into the base of the caecum.

- **Large intestine**: Digestion of cellulose and insoluble carbohydrate occurs in the large intestine, meaning that the horse is a 'hind gut fermenter' (like the rabbit). The caecum and large colon are large, voluminous structures adapted to the fermentation of these carbohydrates. Bacteria ferment the carbohydrate to produce volatile fatty acids, which the horse absorbs and uses as an energy source. One of the by-products of fermentation is gas, which passes out as flatus.

The caecum is a large, comma-shaped, blind-ended fermentation vat that sits mainly on the right side of the abdomen. It has an average length of 3 feet (1 metre) and a capacity of 33 litres. Food can be retained for long periods (several days) in the caecum while fermentation takes place.

The large colon continues from the caecum. It is a long, 'U'-shaped organ that is bent back on itself, making a double horseshoe-shaped loop that is divided into four segments. Three tight bends in the large colon arise where these segments meet each other, and these are termed the sternal, diaphragmatic and pelvic flexures. Although it is only 10-13 feet (3-4 metres) long, it is the largest organ in the abdomen and has an average capacity of 81 litres.

From the large colon, digested food material passes into the small colon, which is much smaller in diameter, and 6.5-13 feet (2-4 metres) long. It absorbs water from the food and forms faecal balls that pass into the rectum and are expelled from the body via the anus.

PERITONEAL CAVITY

The stomach and all of the intestines lie in the peritoneal cavity, in addition to the other abdominal organs (including the liver, spleen, pancreas, bladder and female reproductive tract).

INTESTINAL PROBLEMS

There are a number of peculiarities in the horse's gut that predispose it to disease. These include:

• The inability to vomit means that the horse is prone to a build-up of gas in the stomach (and resulting pain) when very rich carbohydrates are eaten. If

POSITION OF THE INTESTINES IN THE ABDOMEN (AS VIEWED FROM UNDER THE BELLY)

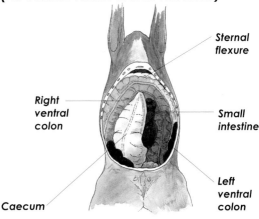

Sternal flexure

Right ventral colon

Small intestine

Left ventral colon

Caecum

there is a severe rise in pressure inside the stomach (which may occur if the small intestine is physically blocked), it may even rupture (which is rapidly fatal).

- The very long small intestine is suspended on a long, thin membrane (the mesentery), which allows it to move around the abdomen. This predisposes it to twisting and other serious problems, resulting in colic.
- Hind gut fermentation can lead to the production of excessive amounts of gas that can accumulate in the gut, causing it to stretch and resulting in pain.
- Much of the large colon lies free in the abdomen (i.e. it is not fixed in its position), which means it can relatively easily move into an abnormal position (displacement) or twist on itself, causing colic.
- The large surface area of the intestines means that diseases that damage the lining can result in the absorption into the blood stream of significant quantities of toxins from inside the gut. The horse is very susceptible to the action of these toxins, and they can cause serious, life-threatening complications (e.g. endotoxic shock, laminitis, kidney failure, etc).
- The normal functioning of the very long intestinal tract requires finely controlled muscular activity that propels food material from the mouth towards the anus. This motility can easily become deranged, which results in pain due to spasm or distension of the bowel wall. Many factors can affect motility, including parasites, dietary changes, etc.

In addition to these peculiarities of the horse's gastrointestinal tract, there are many management factors that play important roles in predisposing horses to colic. The horse evolved as a 'trickle feeder'; i.e. its gastrointestinal tract developed to accept the constant ingestion of herbage throughout the day. Domesticated horses rarely obtain nutrition in this way. The unnatural management and feeding practices that we impose almost certainly predisposes the horse to colic. Several studies have identified particular management or feeding practices that increase the risk of colic. These include:

- Horses fed pelleted feeds and mixed feeds are at an increased risk of colic.
- The risk of colic increases as the quantity of grain fed to horses increases.
- Horses with limited access to grazing are at risk of developing certain forms of colic (e.g. gastric ulcers).
- Horses that are intensively exercised (and fed high-concentrate diets) are at an increased risk of developing gastric ulcers.
- Sudden dietary changes increase the risk of colic.
- Sudden changes in management and exercise increase the risk of colic. For example, horses that are suddenly taken out of exercise and rested are at risk of developing colon impaction.
- Restriction of water intake increases the risk of impaction colic.
- Stress associated with transport, surgery, etc., increases the risk of certain types of colic.
- Feeding immediately after exercise is believed to predispose to colic.

Another major, predisposing factor is a history of previous bouts of colic. Horses with a history of colic are six times more likely to suffer another attack than horses who have never had the condition. Previous abdominal surgery (especially colic surgery) also increases the risk of a horse being affected by colic.

2 Causes of colic

There are numerous causes of colic, and, in the majority of cases, the precise cause remains undetermined. Important causes include:

- Alterations in motility (intestinal dysfunction)
- Tympany
- Simple obstruction
- Strangulation obstruction
- Non-strangulating infarction
- Ulceration
- Enteritis
- Peritonitis

ALTERATIONS IN MOTILITY

Intestinal dysfunction is probably the most common cause of colic. This simply means that part of the bowel is not functioning normally. Many mild bouts of colic are blamed on intestinal spasm (spasmodic colic) or the functional obstruction of the bowel (ileus).

Despite being common, very little is known about this group of diseases. Potential causes include parasite infections, dehydration, electrolyte imbalances, bacterial infections and abnormal intestinal bacterial growth. Some individual horses appear to be prone to motility problems, especially spasmodic colic, and may suffer repeated bouts of mild colic throughout their lives.

TYMPANY

Tympany results from the accumulation of gas within the gastrointestinal tract, causing distension and pain. The parts of the gastrointestinal tract most frequently affected are the stomach, caecum and large colon.

Tympany usually occurs following the ingestion of highly fermentable carbohydrate (such as concentrates or grain), or grazing on lush pasture. Trapped gas causes the stomach or large intestine to expand and results in pain. In severe cases the stomach may even rupture if the pressure within it gets too high.

SIMPLE OBSTRUCTION

Any blockage in the inside of the bowel (lumen) will result in food material and secretions damming up in front of the obstruction, causing the intestine to distend. The resultant stretching of the intestinal wall causes pain. This is accompanied by strong waves of muscular contractions as the body attempts to force food material past the obstruction, which contributes to pain. If the bowel remains distended for a long period of time, damage to the wall occurs, which may subsequently allow bacterial toxins inside the gut lumen to be absorbed into the blood stream. Once in the blood stream, these toxins (endotoxins) result in shock (endotoxic shock), which can be life-threatening.

Simple obstructions may be physical (i.e. a blockage) or functional (i.e. failure of the bowel wall muscles to contract).

Examples of simple physical obstructions include:
• Impaction of food material inside the bowel.
• Foreign bodies stuck inside the bowel.
• Compression of the bowel by a thickening of the intestinal wall (e.g. inflammatory bowel diseases).
• Compression of the bowel by a structure lying against the intestine (e.g. tumour, abscess, adhesion).

Functional obstructions can occur transiently in spasmodic colic, but these usually persist for only a

few seconds or minutes. More persistent functional obstructions (ileus) usually occur secondary to other problems, including:
• Surgical manipulation of the bowel
• Distension of the bowel ahead of a physical obstruction
• Peritonitis
• Grass sickness.

IMPACTIONS
Generally, impactions develop slowly, over a period of many hours to several days. Initially, the horse will show low-grade pain rather than the more severe colic seen with complete obstruction. Faeces may continue to be passed, but they are often reduced in quantity, and may be hard, dry and mucus-covered. Horses with large intestinal impactions are often dull and depressed, with a reduced appetite.

Impactions most frequently occur at the pelvic flexure of the large colon. Causes include:
• Sudden changes in amount of exercise – particularly in horses undergoing enforced rest periods when, previously, they were being regularly exercised (for example, a horse that is box-rested due to lameness).
• Dental problems resulting in inadequate chewing.
• Inadequate water consumption.
• Poor intestinal muscle function due to parasites, previous bowel wall damage, debility, etc.

FOREIGN BODIES
Although relatively rare, foreign bodies in the gut can cause obstruction. For example, horses grazing on sandy soil or turned out into sand schools can ingest large quantities of sand with their food. Over time, sand can accumulate in the bottom of the bowel and cause an obstruction.

ENTEROLITHS

Enteroliths or stones develop inside the intestine. They develop from the precipitation of magnesium salts on to a nidus (an object, usually a foreign body such as a nail or piece of wire) in the intestine. The stones are usually located in the large colon, and may intermittently cause partial obstructions of the intestine. This results in bouts of mild colic resembling colon impactions. However, if the stone moves to a narrower part of the colon, it can cause a complete obstruction, leading to severe colic with the horse rapidly developing shock. Another form of stone is called a bezoar – a ball of plant material (phytobezoar) or hair (trichobezoar).

DISPLACEMENTS

The two arms of the left colon are voluminous and move freely within the abdominal cavity, whereas much of the right colon and caecum are fixed and firmly attached to the body wall. This predisposes the left colon to displacements (movement into an abnormal position) or torsion (twisting of the intestine around itself).

STRANGULATION OBSTRUCTION

Strangulation of the intestine occurs when the blood supply to the affected part is cut off – ischaemia. In effect, ischaemia causes the death of that part of the intestine. In general terms, strangulation obstructions cause severe types of colic with rapidly developing shock. The area affected rapidly degenerates, allowing bacterial toxins (endotoxins) to be absorbed into the general circulation, resulting in endotoxic shock. Horses with strangulation obstructions require surgical treatment, and the diseased segment of bowel will need to be cut out (resected).

EVENTS THAT TAKE PLACE IN SIMPLE AND STRANGULATING OBSTRUCTIONS OF THE INTESTINE

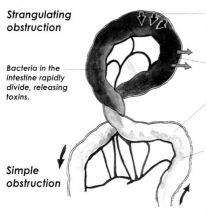

Strangulating obstruction

Bacteria in the intestine rapidly divide, releasing toxins.

Simple obstruction

Haemorrhage occurs in the intestinal wall. The bowel rapidly distends with fluid.

Toxins are rapidly absorbed into the circulation.

The intestine distends with fluid. Eventually, the horse becomes dehydrated.

Persistent distension eventually leads to damage to the intestinal wall, allowing toxins to be absorbed into the circulation.

SMALL INTESTINE

Strangulation obstructions of the small intestine can be caused by a variety of diseases, including entrapment of the intestine in hernias, pedunculated lipomas, intussusceptions and volvulus.

The problem can be further complicated by the effects of ischaemia, which allows endotoxins into the circulation and can lead to endotoxic shock. Shock is much more rapid and severe in strangulation obstructions than it is in simple obstructions. Whereas a horse with a simple obstruction might survive several days without treatment, a horse with a strangulation obstruction would be very unlikely to survive more than 24 hours.

Hernias

Hernias may occur in the body wall (external hernias, e.g. umbilical, inguinal and ventral hernias) or inside the abdominal cavity (internal hernias). Strangulation obstruction in an umbilical hernia is relatively rare,

The surgical view of a strangulated small intestine. The dark-red distended loop of bowel has lost its blood supply (become ischaemic). Above this section of bowel is a distended loop of intestine that has kept its blood supply. Compare these two loops with the normal, empty intestine in the foreground.

despite the fact that umbilical hernias are the most common type of hernia encountered in horses. Inguinal hernias are not uncommon in male foals, but often close spontaneously without treatment, and the intestine rarely strangulates at this age.

Strangulation obstructions of the small intestine in inguinal or scrotal hernias occur occasionally in stallions. A sudden increase in intra-abdominal pressure during breeding, strenuous exercise or abdominal trauma can predispose to inguinal herniation. This type of obstruction should always be suspected in a stallion suffering from severe colic.

Ventral hernias are defects in the lower part of the body wall that are caused by external trauma or surgery. The small or large intestine may become incarcerated in such hernias, although strangulation of the bowel rarely happens.

Pedunculated lipomas

These are a common cause of strangulation obstruction of the small intestine in older horses and ponies. Most affected horses are more than 12 years of age.

Lipomas are benign, fatty growths that develop inside the abdomen, usually originating from the mesentery (the thin veil of tissue that suspends the intestine). They frequently grow on a stalk, so can swing and move around. They can wrap around a segment of small intestine and tighten, causing it to strangulate.

Intussusception

When one section of intestine telescopes into the adjoining section, this causes obstruction of the bowel, which may be partial or complete, depending on how much intestine is involved and how much swelling of the affected bowel wall it produces. The ileum and the junction of the ileum with the caecum are commonly affected, especially in young horses.

Volvulus

This is a form of 'twisted gut', in which a segment of the intestine rotates by 180 degrees or more on its mesentery. The jejunum is usually affected.

LARGE INTESTINE

Strangulation obstruction of the large colon is usually the result of a twist (torsion). Torsions are most common in brood mares around the time of foaling. The twist must be greater than 180 degrees to cause obstruction of the veins draining blood from the colon, and greater than 270 degrees to cause obstruction of the arterial blood supply to the colon. The effects of strangulation obstruction of the colon are similar to that of the small intestine (see above). However, the

Torsion of the large colon, as seen at post-mortem examination.

large surface area of bowel involved in colon torsions results in severe and rapid stagnation of blood in the tissues and rapid absorption of endotoxins into the circulation.

Another, more rare cause of strangulation obstruction of the large intestine is caeco-colic intussusception, in which the caecum telescopes into the large colon. Causes of this include parasite infestations, such as tapeworms and cyathostomes (small redworms).

SMALL COLON
Strangulation obstructions of the small colon are rare. Rupture of the mesentery of the small colon, with subsequent damage to its blood supply and ischaemia, is a rare complication of foaling. Strangulation by pedunculated lipomas (see page 17) can also occur in the small colon.

NON-STRANGULATING INFARCTION
A relatively rare cause of colic, in which the blood supply to various areas of the bowel wall (usually involving the ileum, caecum and/or large colon)

becomes cut off due to a blockage of the blood vessels. Usually, this results from thrombi (clots) that originate in the larger arteries, flow down into smaller arteries, and lodge there. In most cases, thrombi are caused by large redworm larvae. Ischaemia can result from this.

ULCERATION

The stomach contents are normally acidic, due to the secretion of hydrochloric acid in the gastric juice. This acid is potentially harmful to the lining of the stomach (especially the non-glandular part), and there are a number of protective mechanisms that operate to prevent such damage. It is likely that ulceration occurs as a result of an imbalance of these protective mechanisms and the acid production.

Gastric ulceration is very common among foals. Studies suggest that up to 50 per cent of foals have ulcers in the stomach lining. Mostly, these ulcers do not cause symptoms of disease. In mature horses, gastric ulcers are most common among those in race training. Factors predisposing to ulceration include stress, strenuous exercise, lack of grazing, high-concentrate diets, stall confinement, and fasting.

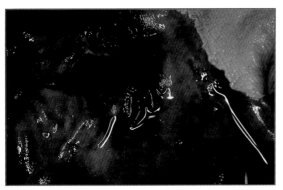

Severe ulceration of the stomach.

ENTERITIS

Enteritis means inflammation of the bowel lining. This can be caused by a wide variety of infectious agents, including bacteria and parasites, as well as certain toxins/poisons. Strictly speaking, enteritis refers to inflammation of the small intestine, which is actually quite rare in adult horses. Enteritis is relatively common in foals, and it is a widely recognised cause of colic in this age group. In adult horses, inflammatory diseases of the caecum, large colon and small colon are much more common than inflammation of the small intestine. Inflammation of the large intestine is called colitis.

Abdominal pain associated with enteritis and colitis is often mild, but the horse may show signs of severe colic if there is marked damage to the internal lining of the bowel. Enteritis in foals and colitis in adult horses is usually accompanied by diarrhoea. However, diarrhoea may not start for several hours, or even a day or two, after the onset of abdominal pain.

Enteritis in foals is usually caused by bacterial or viral infections, including Salmonella, Clostridia, Rotavirus, etc. In adult horses, enteritis is rare. However, one disease, called anterior enteritis (or proximal enteritis) can strike adult horses. It causes inflammation of the duodenum and the first part of the jejunum. The cause is probably a form of Clostridia infection. Anterior enteritis is characterised by the sudden appearance of acute colic, ileus and distension of the stomach with fluid. As such, the disease looks very similar to simple or strangulating obstructions of the duodenum or jejunum.

Colitis in adult horses can be caused by a variety of infections, including the following:

- Clostridia
- Salmonella

- Potomac Horse Fever (in parts of the USA only)
- Cyathostomes (small redworms).

In addition, certain drugs can cause colitis in adults, including some antibiotics and non-steroidal anti-inflammatory drugs (such as phenylbutazone).

PERITONITIS

Peritonitis refers to inflammation of the lining of the abdominal cavity (the peritoneum), usually caused by bacterial infection. This infection can gain access to the abdominal cavity by a variety of routes, including:

- Leakage of bacteria from inside the bowel lumen through an area of damaged or ulcerated bowel wall (for example, strangulated bowel, non-strangulating intestinal infarction, ruptured bowel, etc.).
- Leakage of bacteria from an abscess in the abdomen (for example, following spread of the strangles bacteria to the abdomen – so-called 'bastard strangles').
- Leakage of bacteria from infection in the male/female reproductive tract, or urinary tract.
- Damage or rupture of the uterus or vagina in mares, secondary to trauma from foaling or breeding.
- Wounds to the abdominal wall,
- Contamination of the abdomen occurring at the time of surgery or during various diagnostic procedures.

Regardless of the source of infection, peritonitis in horses usually involves the entire abdominal cavity, and is characterised by the outpouring of fluid and pus into the cavity; this can result in dehydration. The production of inflammatory chemicals in the abdomen causes colic-like pain.

3 Diagnosis of colic

Colic can range from the very mild to the very severe, and it is not always easy to distinguish mild colic from potentially fatal colic. It is important, therefore, that the signs of colic are recognised quickly, and professional veterinary advice is sought early in the course of the disease.

RECOGNISING COLIC

The clinical signs of colic are the behavioural changes that the horse shows as a response to abdominal pain. The severity of these signs varies from mild to severe, depending on the degree of pain.

- Restlessness
- Continuous or intermittent pawing of the ground
- Turning the head round towards the flank
- Kicking with the hind feet at the abdomen
- Crouching as if wanting to lie down
- Repeatedly stretching out into a 'trestle table' stance (as if wanting to urinate but not actually doing so)
- Lying down and getting up repeatedly
- Lying down for excessive periods of time

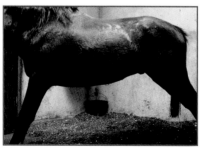

Adoption of the 'trestle table' stance, which can be typical of colic.

- Lying on the back
- Grinding the teeth
- Backing into a corner
- Playing with water or repeatedly putting the head down to water but not drinking
- Biting at the flanks
- Turning and holding the head in an awkward position
- Assuming a 'dog-sitting' position
- Dropping to the ground
- Rolling
- Sweating
- Quivering and repeated curling of the upper lip
- Groaning
- Lack of appetite
- Lack of bowel movements as evidenced by a small number – or absence of – faecal piles
- Passing hard, dry faecal balls, faecal balls covered in slimy mucus, soft faeces or diarrhoea
- Passing abnormally large amounts of flatus
- Distension of the abdomen on one or both sides
- Rapid respiration and/or flared nostrils
- Depression
- Cool extremities.

A horse with colic can show intermittent or continuous signs of being in pain. As a rule, the more severe the disease causing colic, the greater the pain. However, in some cases, the signs of pain may abate in the later stages of the disease. For example, a horse that was showing signs of severe pain, but then calms down and becomes depressed, may appear to be improving. However, it is likely that the horse in this 'stage of indolence' is seriously ill and shocked, and will probably die unless aggressive veterinary treatment is instituted.

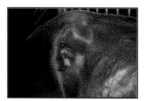

Abrasions over the point of the hip and above the eye can be caused by violent rolling due to colic.

Similarly, a horse found in the morning showing signs of having been in severe colic during the night must be assessed to see if it has recovered or if it is in shock. Signs of this include disturbance of the bed, kick marks on the stable walls, presence of bedding material or dirt in the coat, dried sweat and matting of the coat, and skin abrasions (especially around the eyes and the pelvis).

FALSE COLICS

Not all horses exhibiting signs of abdominal pain will be suffering from a gastrointestinal disease. Other painful conditions can cause similar symptoms. False colics are a group of painful diseases that can produce symptoms very similar to true colic. False colics include diseases of the reproductive tract, liver, kidneys, urinary bladder, muscles, etc. The clinical signs may be indistinguishable from those of a true colic, and careful examination by a veterinary surgeon is important if the correct diagnosis is to be reached.

DIAGNOSING COLIC

In many cases, diagnosing the precise cause of colic is difficult if not impossible. The most important aspect is to decide whether you are dealing with a mild or 'medical' colic, or whether there is a serious and potentially life-threatening disease requiring immediate, intensive therapy or surgery (or even euthanasia).

FIVE CATEGORIES OF COLIC DETERMINED BY DEGREE OF PAIN

NO PAIN
- Normal behaviour and appearance

MILD PAIN
- Occasional pawing
- Occasional turning round to the flank
- Stretching out
- Grinding teeth
- Lying down quietly for long periods

MODERATE PAIN
- Persistent pawing
- Crouching and cramping with attempts to lie down
- Kicking at the abdomen
- Lying down
- Rolling
- Repeated turning round to the flank
- Restlessness

SEVERE PAIN
- Sweating
- Dropping to the ground
- Violent rolling
- Continuous pawing
- Severe restlessness

DEPRESSION
- Quiet and uninterested in environment
- Lack of interest in eating or drinking
- Head held low
- Lying down quietly and reluctant to get up
- Cold and clammy to touch

There are many factors and procedures that the vet will consider when assessing a horse with colic and deciding how it should be treated. These may include some, or all, of the following:

- Clinical history
- Physical examination
- Evidence and nature of pain
- Assessment of shock
- Assessment of bowel activity
- Rectal examination
- Gastric reflux
- Abdominal paracentesis
- Laboratory examinations
- Ultrasound examination
- Endoscopy
- Radiography
- Laparoscopy.

CLINICAL HISTORY

Previous medical problems (particularly previous bouts of colic), feeding, exercise, worming regime and general management should all be considered.

- A horse that has suffered from strangles and recurrent bouts of colic might have an abdominal abscess.
- A horse that develops colic shortly after it has been box-rested might have a colon impaction.
- A stallion with severe colic after covering a mare may have intestinal incarceration in an inguinal hernia.
- A foal or yearling that develops colic shortly after being de-wormed might have an ascarid impaction.
- A horse with colic after being turned out on to lush pasture could have tympanitic colic.

One of the most important factors is the time that has elapsed since the onset of colic. In some cases, the onset will have been observed, and it is, therefore, possible to accurately time the duration of the colic. Unfortunately, in many other cases the time of onset will be unknown. For example, a horse may be found in a state of colic first thing in the morning (having been normal the previous evening), and it is impossible to know at what time during the night the colic started.

PAIN

Pain can be classified as mild, moderate or severe, or the horse may appear depressed. Pain may be different at the time of the examination compared to during the attack. Horses with a strangulating obstruction usually exhibit marked pain for six to eight hours, but after this time, pain may subside. Pain may also be intermittent.

CIRCULATION AND SHOCK

The vet will examine the state of the circulation to look for evidence of shock. Shock can be the result of dehydration and/or the effects of endotoxins in the blood stream. The presence or absence of shock can help determine whether a horse with colic requires surgical treatment. Circulation can be assessed by:

- Heart rate: The normal rate is 30-40 beats per minute. In shock, and as a result of pain, the heart rate increases. Generally, a heart rate greater that 80 beats per minute suggests a severe disease with marked shock; such cases are likely to be fatal unless appropriate (often surgical) treatment is undertaken. The heart rate can be measured by feeling a peripheral arterial pulse (such as the facial artery as it courses over the edge of the lower jaw) or by listening (or feeling) to the heart beat.
- Strength of the arterial pulse.

In a horse suffering from endotoxic shock the mucous membranes (gums) are brick-red in colour.

- Colour of the mucous membranes (e.g. gums and conjunctiva). The colour is pale pink. In hypovolaemic shock, the membranes become more pale and dry. In endotoxic shock, they become brick-red or purple. Terminally, the membranes may turn a pale blue-grey colour.
- The time it takes for colour to return to an area of the gum blanched by finger pressure. This time is known as the 'capillary refill time' and it is normally less than two seconds. In shock, the time becomes prolonged (three seconds or more). In severe shock, the time may be as long as five to six seconds.
- Rectal temperature.

BOWEL ACTIVITY
Assessment of the bowel is made by listening to the abdomen, usually with a stethoscope. Increased sounds may be heard in cases of colitis and in spasmodic colic. Decreased sounds can indicate an obstruction of the bowel. Intestinal sounds are often completely absent within a few hours of a strangulation obstruction.

RECTAL EXAMINATION
In a rectal examination, the veterinarian will insert his or her hand into the horse's rectum, through the anus, in order to assess the abdominal structures in the posterior part of the abdomen. Your vet will discuss

the merits and risks with you before making a decision.

The biggest risk to the horse is inadvertent damage to the wall of the rectum, causing a rectal tear that can result in faecal contamination of the abdomen and subsequent severe (often fatal) peritonitis. To minimise the risk, the horse needs to be restrained. If the examination is being conducted in a stable, the vet may use a twitch or sedation. Both the vet and the person holding the horse must be prepared for sudden movements or attempts by the horse to go down.

In some cases (e.g. impaction of the pelvic flexure), the results of the rectal examination will diagnose the cause of the colic. In other cases, non-specific abnormalities will be identified (such as distension of small intestine), which help determine the possible causes of the colic. In yet other cases, the rectal examination will be normal, thereby eliminating certain possibilities but not positively identifying the cause.

If blood is present on the examiner's arm after the examination, or if blood is passed with faeces after the examination, the possibility of damage to the rectum should be considered. Although rectal tears can be fatal, prompt recognition of the problem and starting appropriate therapy as early as possible will improve the chances of successful treatment.

GASTRIC REFLUX

Passage of a stomach tube is performed in many colic cases to determine whether the stomach is distended with fluid or gas. The stomach tube is passed through the nostril, along the nasal cavity, down the oesophagus, and into the stomach. Reflux of more than 2 litres is considered abnormal and indicates gastric distension. This may occur in small intestinal obstructions, grass sickness, anterior enteritis, peritonitis, etc.

Performing abdominal paracentesis. A hypodermic needle is being carefully pushed into the abdominal cavity from the belly. Fluid is allowed to drip out and can be collected into a blood-collection tube.

ABDOMINAL PARACENTESIS

This procedure, also known as peritoneal tap or abdominocentesis, involves taking a sample of the peritoneal fluid from the abdominal cavity. This can be done by pushing a hypodermic needle, or similar instrument, through the belly wall into the abdominal cavity. This is usually done 'blindly' at the lowest point of the abdomen, but it may also be carried out using ultrasound to guide the placement of the needle.

Normal peritoneal fluid is clear, pale-yellow, watery fluid. In certain diseases, the nature of this fluid can change. For example, in strangulation obstructions of the intestine (see Chapter Two), the fluid often changes colour, becoming orange in the early stages and then red (blood-stained). In peritonitis, the fluid becomes thick and cloudy. Fluid examination can sometimes help to diagnose the underlying disease.

LABORATORY EXAMINATIONS

Routine blood tests are often used to assess the degree of dehydration. More complicated tests, such as blood gas analysis, may be helpful in monitoring intensive therapy in very sick horses. Laboratory tests on peritoneal fluid and faeces are used in some cases, such as suspected peritonitis or parasitic disease.

ULTRASOUND

This technique is particularly useful in the evaluation of foals and yearlings that are too small to have a rectal examination. It can also be helpful in diagnosing certain conditions in adult horses, including intussusceptions and small intestinal distension.

ENDOSCOPY

Endoscopic examination of the stomach is the preferred means of diagnosing gastric ulcers in horses of all ages. In the adult horse, a long endoscope (275-300 cms or 108-118 ins long) is required to reach the stomach. The endoscope is passed in the sedated horse in the same way as a stomach tube.

RADIOGRAPHY

Radiography is of limited value when diagnosing a horse with colic, due to the size of the abdomen and the volume of ingesta in the intestinal tract. However, it can be useful in foals and in diagnosing other diseases (such as enteroliths) in small horses.

LAPAROSCOPY

This involves examination of the abdominal cavity, using a rigid telescope (laparoscope) that is inserted through the body wall. This procedure can be performed in the standing, sedated horse, but it has limited application in horses with acute colic. Its greatest use is in horses with chronic or recurrent colic. Only part of the abdominal cavity can be visualised using this procedure.

4 Treatment

The most commonly used medical treatments
for colic include:
  • Analgesics
• Fluid and electrolytes
• Anti-endotoxin treatments
• Laxatives
• Drugs to alter intestinal motility
• Anti-ulcer drugs.

ANALGESICS

Analgesics are pain-relieving drugs (e.g. phenylbutazone,
flunixin meglumine, xylazine, detomidine, romifidine,
pethidine, morphine, butorphanol, etc.). Some of
these drugs will cause sedation as well as giving pain-
relief. A commonly used drug in the UK is a
combination of a spasmolytic agent (hyoscine) and a
pain-killer (dipyrone), particularly useful for treating
spasmodic colic and colon impactions.

FLUID AND ELECTROLYTES

A horse in severe shock requires intravenous (directly
into the blood stream) administration of balanced
electrolyte solutions, such as saline (sodium and chloride) or Hartmann's solution (containing sodium,
chloride, potassium, lactate and other electrolytes).
These solutions are usually administered through a
catheter into the horse's jugular vein. The amount of
fluid given depends on the degree of dehydration and
the rate of continued fluid loss. Fluid needs to be
replaced quickly to restore the circulation to normal.

Intravenous administration of fluids can help in some cases of colic.

ANTI-ENDOTOXIN AGENTS

Endotoxins enter the circulation when the bowel wall is damaged by distension, poor blood supply, or inflammation. A variety of treatments can be used to inhibit the endotoxins and to counteract their effects:

- Anti-inflammatory drugs (particularly flunixin meglumine)
- Fluid and electrolyte therapy
- Plasma transfusions
- Antiserum against endotoxins.

LAXATIVES

Laxatives soften the faeces and aid their passage along the intestinal tract. They are commonly used to treat impactions of the colon. The two most frequently used are liquid paraffin (mineral oil) and magnesium sulphate (Epsom salts). Liquid paraffin should always be administered via a stomach tube, never into a horse's mouth as it could easily be aspirated into the lungs, where it can cause a fatal pneumonia.

Enemas are solutions administered directly into the rectum to soften the faeces. They are rarely used in adult horses because rectal impactions are uncommon. However, enemas are commonly used in newborn foals to aid the passage of the first droppings (the meconium).

INTESTINAL MOTILITY DRUGS

Spasmolytic drugs (e.g. hyoscine) are useful in the treatment of spasmodic colic. Drugs that increase bowel motility (e.g. metoclopramide, lignocaine, cisapride) are usually used following surgery, when reduction of bowel motility (ileus) can be a problem.

ANTI-ULCER DRUGS

The most effective drugs are those that reduce acid secretion in the stomach (such as cimetidine, ranitidine and omeprazole).

SURGERY

The decision to perform surgery needs to be made promptly, because early surgical treatment is much more likely to be successful than surgery that is delayed. This particularly applies to strangulation obstructions of the intestinal tract. In some cases, examination results will clearly determine if surgery is required, but, in other cases, the vet is left not knowing whether surgery is needed. Then a decision has to be made either to proceed with surgery straight away, or to begin other medical treatment (see above) initially, and then reassess the situation after an appropriate period of time (often one to two hours). In a few cases, a number of repeated re-examinations will be required before deciding to perform surgery.

Surgery is a major undertaking with a number of risks and complications. It is also expensive and involves a lot of intensive, post-operative care. Surgical treatment should, therefore, only be performed if it is deemed absolutely necessary. However, delaying surgery can result in death. It is usually better to perform surgery if there is any indication that it could be required, rather than waiting until it is certain.

APPROPRIATE CASES

Surgery should be recommended:

- When the exact cause of colic has been diagnosed and is known to require surgical treatment (e.g. a permanent obstruction of the intestinal tract).
- When there is no exact diagnosis, but there is enough evidence to suggest that a surgical lesion is probably present.
- When the horse is exhibiting recurrent bouts of colic and a partial intestinal obstruction is suspected.

The following features (alone or in combination) are suggestive that a surgical problem is present:

- Severe, unrelenting pain.
- Pain that recurs rapidly following medical treatment (i.e. within one to two hours of analgesic treatment).
- Shock or progressive deterioration of the state of the circulation.
- Positive findings on rectal examination.
- Significant volumes of gastric reflux on passage of a stomach tube.
- Changes in the appearance of the peritoneal fluid (orange or red discoloration).
- Progressive abdominal distension.

Response to medical treatment is often an important determining factor when no specific diagnosis has been made at the initial examination. There are many different pain-killing drugs (analgesics – see above) that are used in the treatment of colic. These drugs vary in their potency and action, and must be chosen carefully in cases where the diagnosis is uncertain. Pain that recurs following the use of a pain-killer is an important finding that could sway the veterinary surgeon to deciding that the horse has a surgical problem. It is important, therefore, that very potent drugs that might mask this pain (and other signs, such as those associated with the absorption of endotoxins) are not used initially to treat horses with colic of undetermined origin.

PREFORMING SURGERY

Once the decision has been made that the horse is to undergo surgery, it should be transported to the nearest equine hospital that has expertise in colic surgery as soon as possible. In addition to the university veterinary schools, there are now several private equine hospitals around the country that routinely undertake colic surgery. It is important that the horse is sent somewhere where expertise (both in terms of the surgery and the after-care) is available. Prior to transport, several measures should be taken to stabilise the horse's condition. These include:

- Passage of a stomach tube to decompress the stomach
- Administration of adequate analgesic drug therapy
- If the horse is in shock, intravenous fluid therapy might be undertaken
- Administration of an antibiotic
- Rug the horse up and bandage its limbs.

The hospital should be provided with an accurate report of all treatments administered, and the driver should be sure of the directions to the hospital. An estimated time of arrival should be provided to the hospital.

5 Prevention and management

There are numerous causes of colic, and many cannot be prevented. However, management and dietary factors also play important roles, and this is an area where we can take positive action.

PREVENTION

- Establish a regular feeding and exercise routine.
- Feed a high-quality diet with as much roughage as possible. Hay should usually be available ad lib.
- Feed as little concentrate feed and grain as practical. At least 60 per cent of the horse's daily energy requirement should be in the form of hay or forage.
- Feed hay and water before grain or concentrates.
- Do not feed/water horses immediately after exercise.
- Restrict access to highly fermentable carbohydrates, such as lush grass.
- Daily concentrates should be fed in two or more small feeds, rather than one large meal.
- Provide daily exercise and/or turnout.
- Do not confine a horse to a stall/stable for more than 12 hours per day.
- Provide clean water at all times. Make sure that the water supply does not freeze over in cold weather.
- Establish a strict parasite-control strategy.
- Do not over-graze pastures.
- Perform regular dental check-ups.
- Avoid very coarse hay, especially for old, miniature horses/ponies, and those with dental problems.
- Check pasture/hay/bedding for toxic plants and foreign material.

- Never feed mouldy hay, grain or concentrates.
- Do not feed from the ground, especially on sandy soil.
- Reduce stress as much as possible. Changes should be done slowly. Take special care when horses are transported or moved to a new environment.
- If change in exercise or stabling is unavoidable (e.g. a horse that has to be box-rested because of lameness), the concentrate ration should be reduced and the horse fed a more laxative diet (e.g. bran mashes).
- Only give medication prescribed by your vet.
- Maintain accurate records of health, management, feeding, de-worming, etc.

MANAGING COLIC

Knowing what to do and when can play a direct role in saving the life of a horse that develops colic.

IMMEDIATE ACTION

Time is a critical factor in treating colic successfully. Most horses will recover with very simple treatments, but some require intensive treatment and/or surgery. The earlier the diagnosis, the better the chance of survival.

If you suspect that your horse has colic:

❶ Remove all food and water. Prevent the horse from eating bedding if he tries to do so.

❷ Inform your veterinary surgeon immediately.

❸ Have the following information ready for the vet:
  - Behavioural signs of colic and severity of pain.
  - Pulse (heart) rate.
  - Colour of mucous membranes.
  - Bowel sounds or lack of them.
  - Consistency and frequency of faeces.
  - Recent changes in management, diet or exercise.
  - Medical history, including previous colic episodes.
  - De-worming history.

❹ Walk the horse slowly around, if it is possible and safe to do so. However, do not exhaust the horse or force it to walk if it is reluctant.

❺ If the horse is too violent to walk, allow it to lie down and roll, making sure that it cannot injure itself.

❻ Do not administer any drugs unless specifically directed to do so by your veterinary surgeon.

❼ Follow your vet's advice until he or she arrives.

AFTER CARE

Following resolution of colic signs, the horse must be monitored carefully for any recurrence of pain. Particular attention should be paid to the following:

• General attitude and behaviour
• Water intake and urination frequency
• Gut sounds and passage of faeces and gas
• Mucous membrane colour.

Warm, clean water should be available, and it is important that the horse drinks adequate quantities. If the horse is reluctant to drink, a bucket of water can be flavoured with salt (one tablespoon per 3 gallons), an electrolyte mixture, molasses, or apple juice.

Bran mashes are an excellent feed for horses following colic. However, some horses refuse to eat mashes, in which case they may be made more palatable by mixing in chopped carrots or apples, or mixing with molasses. Mashes can be fed three to four times a day. The horse should be seen to pass several piles of droppings before hay is gradually re-introduced. Ideally, grain or concentrates should not be fed for two to three days after a bout of colic.

Short periods of walking help to improve normal bowel activity, as well as the horse's attitude. Allowing short grazing periods during walks is also beneficial.

6 Grass sickness

Grass sickness is a disease of the nervous tissues that control the bowel. Although it is most common in the north-east of Scotland, the disease has been recognised throughout the UK as well as in many other northern European countries.

There are three forms of grass sickness (acute, sub-acute, and chronic), although there is some overlap between them. The disease is characterised by difficulty in swallowing and varying degrees of immotility of the gastrointestinal tract. The acute and sub-acute forms of the disease are invariably fatal. However, some mildly affected horses may survive. Despite extensive research, the precise cause remains unknown.

The disease is most common among two- to seven-year-olds, mainly in the spring and summer months, especially between April and July. As the name implies, grass sickness is almost exclusively a disease of grazing horses. It is extremely rare in housed animals. Occasionally, a strong association exists with certain premises, and many cases occur in animals that have moved to a new pasture within the preceding few weeks. Cool (7-10 degrees C or 44-50 degrees F), dry weather tends to occur 10-14 days before outbreaks.

The cause of grass sickness is unknown, but it seems likely that a natural poison or toxin on the pasture is responsible. Investigation into the possible role of toxic plants, viruses, fungal, chemical and bacterial toxins has failed to identify the cause. Current evidence suggests that a toxin produced by Clostridia bacteria (a form of botulism) may be involved.

CLINICAL SIGNS

ACUTE

The onset and progression of clinical signs in the acute form is rapid, with death occurring in less than 48 hours. The clinical signs include:

- Depression
- Inappetence
- Colic
- Rapid heart rate (may exceed 100 beats per minute)
- Drooping of the upper eyelids
- Muscle tremors (especially over shoulders and thighs)
- Sweating (whole body or localised to the flanks, neck and shoulder regions)
- Difficulty in swallowing food and water (many cases will flick their muzzle through the water or 'paw' at the water bucket, presumably through frustration)
- Excessive dribbling of saliva
- Spontaneous gastric reflux with foul-smelling green or brown fluid exiting from both nostrils (in those that do not show spontaneous reflux, passage of a stomach tube will invariably result in the retrieval of many litres of malodorous reflux)
- Abdominal distension.

The clinical signs and results of rectal examination can appear similar to those encountered in some cases of surgical colic caused by an obstruction in the small intestine. The prognosis in acute cases is hopeless, and euthanasia is advised.

SUB-ACUTE

Sub-acute cases present similarly to, but less severe than, acute cases. The duration of clinical signs is longer and the abdomen quickly develops a marked,

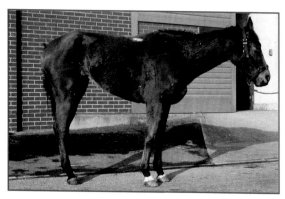

The severe weight loss and tucked-up appearance seen in this horse is typical of sub-acute and chronic grass sickness.

'tucked-up' appearance. As the disease progresses, many sub-acute cases will exhibit worsening episodes of colic due to colonic impaction. A small number of cases that present initially as sub-acute cases will gradually progress to the chronic stage, but the vast majority will die or need euthanasia within seven days.

CHRONIC

The clinical signs in the chronic form are more insidious in onset. Typical signs include:

- Severe weight loss with the development of a distinct 'tucked up' abdomen (see above)
- A characteristic 'elephant-on-a-tub' posture (all four feet placed close together)
- Drooping of the upper eyelids resulting in a sleepy and/or depressed expression
- Rapid heart rate (but rarely exceeding 60 beats per minute)
- Muscle tremors
- Patchy sweating
- Colic (usually mild and transient)

- Difficulty in swallowing (but the associated reduction in appetite can make this difficult to appreciate)
- Accumulation of chewed food between the cheeks and molar teeth resulting in an unpleasant odour to the breath
- 'Snuffling' sound during breathing that originates from the nasal cavity, which accumulates a thick, sticky secretion.

DIAGNOSIS

Confirmation diagnosis of grass sickness can be made in one of two ways:
- Finding the characteristic lesions in the nerves at post-mortem examination
- Biopsy of the ileum obtained during surgery.

The latter technique can be useful in the diagnosis of acute and sub-acute cases where surgical colic is a major differential diagnosis. In chronic cases, however, where subsequent treatment is being considered, anaesthesia and surgery are likely to adversely affect the outcome.

As a result of this, diagnosis of most cases is made on clinical signs and history. Other techniques that may aid diagnosis include endoscopy and contrast radiography of the oesophagus.

TREATMENT

Only chronic cases can be considered for treatment. The following features should be present if treatment is to be attempted:
- Some ability to swallow
- A degree of intestinal motility
- Absence or mild/intermittent symptoms of colic only

- Some appetite
- Pulse rate less than 60 beats per minute.

Nursing care is the most important aspect of treatment. The use of palatable, high-energy, high-protein feed is recommended, although the animal should be tempted to eat whatever it wants. The horse should be offered food at least four to five times a day. Preferred feeds include crushed oats and high-energy cubes. Soaking the feed may facilitate swallowing in some cases. The energy content of the feed may be improved by the addition of up to 500ml (17 fluid ounces) of corn oil, but this should be done gradually. Palatability can be improved by mixing in dilute molasses or succulents, such as cut grass, carrots or apples. The importance of nursing, frequent human contact, frequent grooming, and regular walking out and hand grazing cannot be over-emphasised.

Drugs to stimulate intestinal motility may also be used in some cases. Pain-killers are given as necessary.

PREVENTION

Although no guaranteed methods of prevention are known, certain precautions can be taken to reduce the risk of grass sickness. This is particularly relevant during the high-risk season (March to July). Preventative measures include housing new arrivals for a two-month period before turnout, avoiding any change in pasture during the high-risk season, and avoiding the use of pasture where the disease has occurred before. In high-risk areas, housing the horse may also be advisable if the prior 7-10 days have been cool and dry.

7 Colic in the foal

Diagnosing and treating colic in the foal requires slightly different methods to that of the adult horse. It relies largely on a thorough assessment of the animal's history and a full physical examination. In some cases, diagnostic aids (e.g. ultrasound and radiographs) will be helpful.

HISTORY

Normal parameters for newborn foals are:

TIME TO SUCKLING REFLEX	Normally within 20 minutes
TIME TO STANDING	Average 57 minutes
TIME TO NURSING FROM MARE	Average 111 minutes

In general, a foal that is not able to stand and nurse by two hours should be considered potentially abnormal.

Adequate intake of colostrum (first milk) is essential. Failure to ingest adequate amounts will increase its susceptibility to infectious causes of colic (enteritis).

The foal's age can be helpful in determining the cause of colic. For example, foals with meconium impactions usually present within 12-36 hours of birth with a distended abdomen and failure to pass meconium (first faeces). Foals with rupture of the bladder usually present at three days of age, with depression, a distended abdomen and/or abnormalities with urination.

PHYSICAL EXAMINATION

Valuable information can be gained by simply observing the foal. Restrained foals often cannot, or will not, display true signs of colic. Nursing behaviour can also be observed (e.g. a foal that nurses, only to detach from the teat early and then retreat to grind its teeth and salivate, might be suffering from gastric ulceration).

If a foal is straining, the veterinarian will need to establish if it is straining to defecate or urinate. Straining to defecate is characterised by an arched back (convex shape) and elevated tail, while straining to urinate is characterised by spread legs, sunken back (concave shape) and tail elevation.

The age of the foal must be taken into consideration when evaluating the results of the clinical examination.

Age	Heart rate (beats per min)	Respiratory rate (breaths per min)	Temperature (degrees C/F)	Capillary refill time (seconds)
Newborn	• 40-80 (at birth) • 130-150 (trying to stand) • 70-100 (first day)	• 60-80 (first hour) • 20-40 (first day)	• 37.2-38.9 C (99-102 F)	• <2
7 days	• 70-100	• 20-40	• 38-39 C (100-102 F)	• <2
3 months	• 30-60	• 12-20	• 37.5-38.5 C (99-101 F)	• <2

MECONIUM RETENTION

Meconium retention is one of the most common causes of abdominal pain and distension in very young foals. Meconium pellets can be quite firm and dry, and often lead to difficulty in passage through the newborn foal's narrow pelvis and rectum. Colts are thought to be more commonly affected than fillies, because of their relatively smaller pelvic size.

Foals should begin to pass their meconium within a few hours of birth. Typical signs of retention include straining to defecate, colic, and abdominal distension. Palpation of the rectum with a finger will often reveal retained meconium. Radiography can be helpful.

Treatment involves pain-killers, enemas and liquid paraffin. In most cases, meconium will pass within a matter of a few hours, and is followed by the passage of the first true 'milk' faeces, which are pale and soft.

ENTERITIS

Enteritis is common among foals, with causes including 'foal heat diarrhoea', and viral and bacterial infections. Diarrhoea is diagnostic, but some foals may present with acute colic before diarrhoea has developed. Such cases can be difficult to distinguish from surgical colics. Ultrasound examination and radiography can help to distinguish enteritis from surgical cases of colic.

The treatment of enteritis is medical, and may include fluid and electrolyte therapy, plasma and antibiotics, anti-ulcer therapy, anti-diarrhoea medication, and pain relief.

RUPTURED BLADDER

Uroperitoneum (the accumulation of urine in the abdominal cavity) is a cause of abdominal distension in foals, caused by urine leaking from the urinary tract into the abdomen. Colts are more commonly affected.

Clinical signs may not develop for two to three days following birth, but include progressive abdominal distension, depression, and decreased interest in nursing. Straining to urinate is also commonly observed, and affected foals may show signs of mild colic. Treatment involves surgical repair.

GASTRIC ULCERATION

Gastric ulceration is common in foals, although it is mild in most cases, and the affected foals show few, if any, untoward effects of the disease. In such cases of 'silent ulceration', there are no clinical signs to indicate that the foal has ulcers. In other, more severe cases, clinical signs will be observed, which include:

- Colic
- Poor nursing
- Teeth grinding and/or salivation
- Lying on the back
- Depression
- Diarrhoea
- Chronic poor condition.

Diagnosis is made by endoscopic examination. Treatment includes the use of anti-ulcer medication.

VOLVULUS OF THE SMALL INTESTINE

A length of small intestine, ranging from a few centimetres to several metres, may be twisted or knotted. Volvulus is seen most often in foals younger than three months, and may be a result of changing feeding habits as the foal adapts to digesting bulkier adult food. Pain may seem to fluctuate, but quickly becomes severe. Treatment is surgical.

ASCARID IMPACTION

The roundwom *Parascaris equorum* may cause intestinal obstruction, especially in weanlings (average age five months). Affected foals usually appear unthrifty, and impaction often follows de-worming treatment. If large numbers of roundworms accumulate in the ileum, impaction and subsequent obstruction of the bowel can result. Treatment involves their surgical removal.